Poems From The Playroom

Dawn Potter

For Bethany and Danny

With grateful thanks to my family and friends for all their support and help with this book, especially Darran, Mum, Duncan, Kelly, Claire and Mark.

Text & Illustrations copyright © Dawn Potter 2004

Pandy's Pattern copyright © Marian Parsons 2004
(my wonderful Auntie and kindred spirit)

Published by Dawn Potter
First published in 2004

1 3 5 7 9 10 8 6 4 2

ISBN 0-9546717-0-8

Contents

Rusty	7
Rosie Red Lips	9
Pyjama Ted	13
Dog-on-Wheels	15
Trelawney	17
Little Ed	21
Cotton Puff	23
The Budgie Scout	25
Sandy Brown	27
Ellie's Library	29
Pandy	33
Pandy's Pattern	34

Rusty

Lots of toys make noises,
Dollies even wail,
Teddies have a growler
And me – I have my tail.

A silly place, I hear you say,
From which a toy should speak,
But give my tail a little squeeze
And you will hear a squeak.

The children come and find me,
They think it's rather neat
To sit and pat my bottom
And make a squeaky beat.

I wear a knitted jumper
As my seams began to fray,
But still my fur is wearing thin
From all the constant play.

My tail is feeling sore now
And its squeezebox needs a rest,
So you won't see Rusty for a while
I'm hiding in this chest!

Rosie Red Lips

My real name is Rosanna
A pretty name I think,
But I'm known as Rosie Red Lips
How I wish my lips were pink.

My hair is thick and wavy
A shade of honey brown,
I love my golden tresses
But my lips they let me down.

My eyes are blue and sparkle
Like sapphires under light,
My eyebrows thin and subtle
But my lips are much too bright.

I wear a lovely outfit
In a dainty pastel print,
It compliments my skin tone
A flawless peachy tint.

I know I should be happy
My maker did her best,
Just didn't choose a lipstick
That matches all the rest!

But I'm really rather lucky
As with lips you cannot miss,
Whenever children pick me up
I always get a kiss!

Pyjama Ted

Can I tell you a secret?
There's something no-one knows,
I like my bedtime outfit
But I need some other clothes.
Perhaps a pair of denim jeans,
Green jumper and a hat,
Or even a bright red football kit
Oh how good I'd look in that!
I'd like to go out with the children,
But they call me Pyjama Ted
And as these night clothes are all I wear
They keep me tucked up in bed.

Dog-on-Wheels

I'd love a run in the country
Or even a stroll in the park,
I'd be on my best behaviour
And I'd promise not to bark.

Perhaps we could find the coastal path
And follow the steps to the sea,
Digging sand and jumping waves
Oh such a happy dog I'd be!

Then into the woods for fun and games,
There's so many sticks to chew,
Lots of rabbits to chase around
And those cheeky squirrels too!

The meadow grass so thick and tall
Would make such a great place to hide,
I'd disappear in the undergrowth
Then jump, when called, to your side.

But all these places I'll never see,
I just dream of playing a game,
For I only go wherever I'm pushed
As I'm screwed to this rusty old frame.

The walk I get is the same each day,
Across the playroom floor ...
Past the bookcase, around the chair
And SMASH into the cupboard door!

Trelawney

Tigers should be fearless,
Tigers should be bold,
Tigers should look stunning
With stripes of black and gold.
I used to like adventures
And finding places new,
I was known as Great Trelawney
A tiger brave and true.
But time has changed this tiger,
Now I stay at home instead
And never venture very far
From my soft green blanket bed.

My stripes are not so
            striking,

They've faded pink
        and grey,

Now,

    "YAWNEY
    TRELAWNEY"

        the tiger,

Just snoozes the day
      away ……

Little Ed

In the corner of the playroom
Sat a wool plush little ted,
To all her friends and playmates
She was simply known as 'Ed'.
"Must be short for Eddie!"
The children all exclaimed,
"Or maybe even Edward
Do you think that's what he's named?"
Ed just sat there listening
They were never going to guess,
So she reached into the toy box
And pulled out a pretty dress.
She put it on and looked so sweet
You really should have seen her,
The children smiled and knew at once
Her real name was Edwina.

Cotton Puff

It's the colour of sherbet, marshmallows too,
All sweet and sugary, a real treat for you.

The colour of candy floss, held on a stick,
Making such a sticky mess when you take a lick.

The colour of spring blossom covering the trees,
The colour of a fragrant rose attracting summer bees.

The colour of a baby's dress, edged in pretty lace,
The colour of a cotton puff for powdering your face.

It's such a lovely colour, so many people think,
But I know that a rabbit just doesn't suit pink!

The Budgie Scout

I get a good view of the playroom
From high on my pencil perch,
So should any things go missing,
It's me who leads the search.

I'm always going hunting
For those little items we lose,
Part of a jigsaw, a tiddlywink,
Or one of Rosie's shoes.

Because I'm so small and agile
I can check each cranny and nook,
I swoop under beds and into drawers,
There's nowhere I can't look!

My beady eyes are sharp and keen
Through the dark and dusk they seek,
Until I find that missing piece
And clench it in my beak.

I'm careful not to drop it
So I cannot say a word,
Until I reach the toy chest
What a clever bird!

Then with a triumphant little tweet
I let it fall away,
Back with all the other toys
Ready for lots more play.

Finding all those treasured things
That's what it's all about,
So should you lose a special toy
Just tell the Budgie Scout.

Sandy Brown

I'm not a palomino,
A chestnut or a bay,
I'm not a dun or piebald
Or even a dappled grey.

I'm not a working shire horse
With pretty plaited mane,
I've no wooden cart to pull
Along the farmer's lane.

I'm not a racing filly
There's no jockey on my back,
Just a red felt saddle
And ribbons for my tack.

I'm not a fancy fairground horse
Bobbing up and down ...

I'm just the playroom pony,

Plain,
      old,
            Sandy Brown.

Ellie's Library

What type of book do you enjoy
Before you go to bed?
Pages of fact or fiction,
Or poetry instead?

There are many books to choose from
Up on the playroom shelf,
Just let me reach one with my trunk
And have a look yourself.

Perhaps a tale of pirates
Who sailed the seven seas,
Or maybe an animal alphabet
To learn your ABCs.

A fairytale with sad princess
Who longs for love and laughter,
But when the handsome prince arrives
She'll live happily ever after.

There's even a book on dinosaurs
Who lived so long ago,
Filled with facts and figures
And all you want to know.

Because us elephants "never forget"
I remember every book,
My library has something for everyone
So come and take a look!

Pandy

Do you sometimes wonder?
Has it ever crossed your mind?
Could there be a special use
For odd balls of wool you find?

Leftover black from Grandad's socks,
White from a baby's shawl,
A little blue from a bobble hat,
Have they any use at all?

Yes you only need a little time
And some needles (number three),
Just follow "Pandy's Pattern"
And knit them into me!

Pandy's Pattern

Follow these instructions to knit your very own Pandy!

Materials
Oddments of blue, black and white wool of a similar thickness. Small amount of washable toy stuffing. One pair 3mm needles and a spare needle.

Abbreviations
st(s) = stitch(es); alt = alternate; inc = increase by working into front and back of stitch; dec = decrease by working two stitches together.

Note
Work all pieces in garter stitch (all knit rows).

Legs and Body - make 2

*Cast on 6 sts with blue for shoe. Knit 1 row. Inc 1 st at each end of next and following alt row (10 sts). Knit 12 rows.

Join black and knit 1 row. Inc 1 st at each end of next row (12 sts). Knit 14 rows straight. Break yarn and leave sts on spare needle. Repeat from * for right leg.

Joining row - knit across sts of right leg and then across sts on spare needle for left leg (24 sts). Knit 1 row. Join blue for shorts and knit 16 rows.

Join white and knit 4 rows. Dec 1 st at each end of next 6 rows (12 sts). Knit 6 rows. Cast off.

Arms – make 2

Cast on 6 sts with black. Knit 1 row. Inc 1 sts at each end of next and every alt row until there are 14 sts. Knit 8 rows straight.

Dec 1 st at each end of next and every alt row until 6 sts remain. Knit 1 row. Cast off.

Ears – make 2

Cast on 10 sts with black. Knit 4 rows. Dec 1 st at each end of next and every alt row until 4 sts remain. Knit 3 rows. Inc 1 st at each end of next and every alt row until there are 10 sts. Knit 4 rows. Cast off.

Head

Cast on 24 sts with white. Knit 1 row. Inc 1 st at each end of every row until there are 40 sts. Knit 2 rows (mark each end of last row with a coloured thread). Dec 1 st at each end of every row until 28 sts remain. Dec 1 st at each end of every alt row until 2 sts remain. Knit 2 sts together and fasten off.

To make up

With right sides of work together join all seams of legs and body leaving white edges open. Turn right side out and stuff. Join shoulder and neck seams.

Join edge of head together from cast on row to coloured marker. Bring cast off point to coloured marker to form nose and join seams. Turn right side out and stuff. Sew neck edge to body, gathering slightly if required.

Join cast on and cast off edges of arms together. Join one side seam. Turn right side out and stuff.
Sew arms to body.

Join row ends of ears together. Turn right side out and stuff. Sew ears to head. Using black wool embroider eyes and nose as in picture.

Dawn Potter was born in 1967 and lives in Kent with her husband and two children.

She has been a successful artist teddy bear maker under the name of *Willow Bears* and now co-owns *The Old Playroom* - a small shop specialising in antique and collectable toys located in West Malling.

She is the author, illustrator and publisher of this, her first book.

www.dawnpotter.com